Elizabeth, Who is <u>NOT</u> a Saint

By

Kathleen C. Szaj

Illustrated by

Mark A. Hicks

Paulist Press
New York/Mahwah, N.J.

D1413595

Library of Congress Cataloging-in-Publication Data

Szaj, Kathleen C.
    Elizabeth, who is not a saint / by Kathleen C. Szaj; illustrated by Mark A. Hicks.
      p. cm.
    Summary: Grandmother helps Elizabeth understand that she can best express her strong spirit, not by getting in trouble with inappropriate words and actions, but by doing things that she likes and feeling proud of herself.
    ISBN 0-8091-6638-0 (alk. paper)
    [1. Behavior—Fiction. 2. Self-esteem—Fiction. 3. Grandmothers—Fiction.] I. Hicks, Mark A., ill. II. Title.
    PZ7.S9858E1 1997
    [E]—dc21   97-1682
                                              CIP
                                             AC

Published by Paulist Press
997 Macarthur Boulevard
Mahwah, New Jersey 07430

Printed and bound in the
United States of America

To the irrepressible
Elizabeth Starr Naiden

for Kelsey
M.A.H.

Jennifer is a little saint, my Aunt Louise tells me, because there's hardly a peep out of her the whole time the grown-ups talk and talk. Little saints, Aunt Louise says, NEVER interrupt to say they have to have a glass of juice (apple, not orange) RIGHT NOW or to tell their mothers they want a pair of new shoes (without bows or straps) right away or to send their visitors home before they've even had dinner.

Not like
Elizabeth,
who peeps
and squeaks
and shrieks
whenever
guests come . . .
and who
certainly
is NOT a
little saint.

Brian is a perfect gentleman, my Grandpa Joe tells me, because he says his pleases and thank-yous BEFORE he's told to and because he offers to help carry home the groceries (even the bag with the broccoli in it) and because he says "Excuse me" right after he burps.

Perfect gentlemen and perfect ladies, says Grandpa Joe,
NEVER crawl under the table during dinner in restaurants

or spit into their mothers' ears instead of
kissing them good night

or tell their Aunt Louise that
the new casserole she made for
lunch looks really disgusting.
Not like Elizabeth, who won't
touch broccoli OR casseroles
with a ten-foot pole . . . and
who definitely is NOT
a perfect lady.

Tasha is the sweetest angel,
my baby-sitter tells me, because she
ALWAYS waits until a grown-up finishes talking on the
telephone before asking for a snack (please) and brushes her
teeth with REAL toothpaste after dinner and only has to be
told TWICE that it's her bedtime.

A sweet angel, my baby-sitter says,
NEVER galumphs around the
house like a two-ton elephant
when she's supposed to
be quiet as a mouse
or screams bloody
murder when she's
getting her hair
combed or calls
her baby-sitter
"stupid."

Not like Elizabeth, who starts stomping and
screaming extra loud as soon as the telephone
rings . . . and who is almost never (except maybe
when she is sleeping) a sweet angel.

Not like Elizabeth, who jumped on her mother's bed until her mother nearly went crazy AND who said "No way, José" when Grandpa Joe asked to talk with her on the telephone

AND who cut her new red party dress with her
mother's sharp scissors to make the sleeves shorter.

Not like me, who was sent to my room for being a nuisance, a rude child and a brat all day on the same day that my Grandma Sophia came for a visit.

Grandma came to my room and said she'd heard I was getting myself into a lot of trouble lately.

I told her to go away, but she said she would go only after we talked.

I said okay, but only for a minute.

Grandma said she thought maybe she knew what the real trouble was.

I said the real trouble is that I am NOT a little saint like Jennifer or a perfect lady like Brian is a perfect gentleman or hardly ever a sweet angel like Tasha (except maybe when I'm sleeping).

The trouble, Grandma said, is that I have a strong spirit inside me.

Big deal, I told my grandma.

Grandma
said having a strong
spirit is a VERY big deal because it makes a person like me feel
hurt or happy, disappointed or angry, or whatever she feels extra
strong and extra long.

I asked Grandma if a strong spirit can get a little girl into
lots of trouble. She said yes, it can if the girl (or boy) doesn't
help this spirit by giving it some rules and reminders.

I asked Grandma if my strong spirit got me into trouble when I said my Aunt Louise's casserole looked disgusting. She said it probably did, especially if I didn't remind myself not to hurt Aunt Louise's feelings before I said anything. Hurting people's feelings, my Grandma Sophia said, is NOT a good way to use a strong spirit.

I asked Grandma if my spirit gets me into trouble when I scream bloody murder while my baby-sitter is trying to comb my hair. She said yes, it could, especially if I didn't show my baby-sitter where I put my soft hairbrush so she wouldn't have to use the hard comb. Screaming at people, my Grandma Sophia said, is NOT a good way to show a strong spirit.

How about jumping on my mother's bed or cutting the sleeves of my new dress? That's when Grandma said that she thought driving my mother crazy is NOT a good way to share my strong spirit.

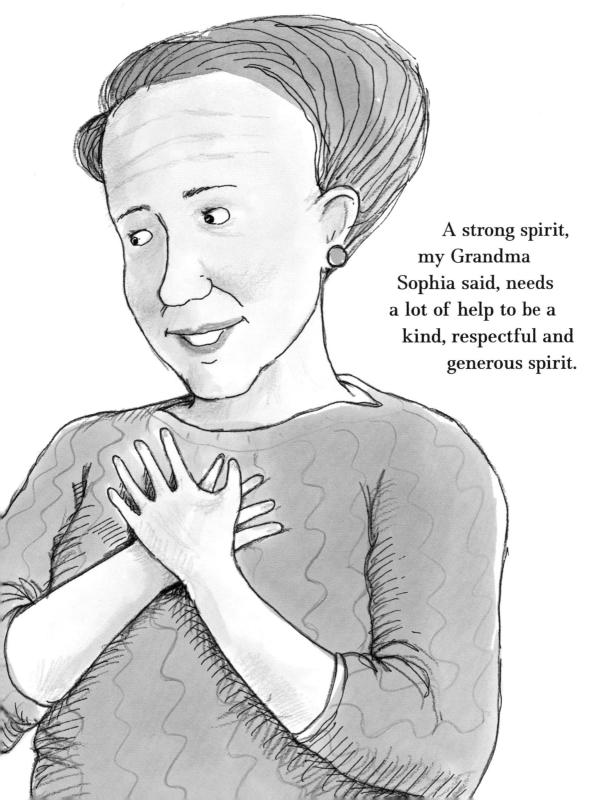

A strong spirit,
my Grandma
Sophia said, needs
a lot of help to be a
kind, respectful and
generous spirit.

I told my grandma, "But I don't know HOW to help my strong spirit."

"Oh, but you do, my Elizabeth," Grandma answered.

"Well," I said, "maybe I do, but I need a clue."

Grandma
suggested that
I think of the
things that
I make or do
that make me feel
especially good about myself.
    I thought and thought . . . so hard
I think I felt my brain get squished.

"How about when I draw my pictures
of worms with polka dots and stripes using
lots of great colors?" I asked.

"That's good," said Grandma.
"What else?"

"How about when I make up stories to act out, like the one where we pretended I was a giant chicken and you were a lizard monster (that ate giant chickens)?"

"Definitely," said Grandma. "What else?"

"How about when I sing 'Do-re-mi' backward and forward or 'On Top of Spaghetti' with all the verses—and no one is listening except me?

Or, when I make my OWN peanut butter, banana and catsup sandwich (and even remember to put it on a plate)?"

"Bingo!" Grandma said. She told me that each time I do or make something I really like for myself or someone else, I am helping my spirit to be strong in ways that I can feel proud of myself.

Then my grandma
shared a secret about
herself that I am
sure I already
knew.

I'm glad I have a strong spirit inside me, even if it does mean getting myself into real trouble sometimes.

Because now I can be just Elizabeth, who will never EVER be a little saint . . . or a big one, either.

That's a VERY big deal, you know. Just ask my Grandma Sophia.